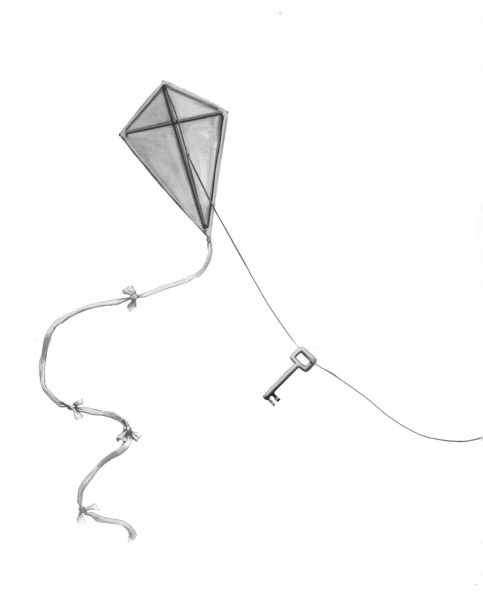

NATIONAL GEOGRAPHIC
WASHINGTON, D.C.

NATIONAL
GEOGRAPHIC
KiDS

BENJAMIN FRANKLIN'S
WISE WORDS

HOW TO
WORK SMART,
PLAY WELL,
AND MAKE REAL FRIENDS

K. M. KOSTYAL

ILLUSTRATED BY FRED HARPER
WITH A FOREWORD BY FRANKLIN BIOGRAPHER H. W. BRANDS

Text copyright © 2017 K.M. Kostyal
Illustrations copyright © 2017 Fred Harper
Compilation copyright © 2017 National Geographic Partners, LLC

All rights reserved. Reproduction of the whole or any part of the contents
without written permission from the publisher is prohibited.

Since 1888, the National Geographic Society has funded more than 12,000
research, exploration, and preservation projects around the world. The Society
receives funds from National Geographic Partners, LLC, funded in part by your
purchase. A portion of the proceeds from this book supports this vital work.
To learn more, visit www.natgeo.com/info.

For more information, visit nationalgeographic.com, call 1-800-647-5463,
or write to the following address:
National Geographic Partners
1145 17th Street N.W.
Washington, D.C. 20036-4688 U.S.A.

Visit us online at nationalgeographic.com/books

For librarians and teachers: ngchildrensbooks.org

More for kids from National Geographic: kids.nationalgeographic.com

For information about special discounts for bulk purchases, please contact
National Geographic Books Special Sales: ngspecsales@ngs.org

For rights or permissions inquiries, please contact National Geographic Books
Subsidiary Rights: ngbookrights@ngs.org

NATIONAL GEOGRAPHIC and Yellow Border Design are trademarks
of the National Geographic Society, used under license.

Production design by David M. Seager
Art direction and design by Amanda Larsen

Hardcover ISBN: 978-1-4263-2699-8
Reinforced Library Binding ISBN: 978-1-4263-2700-1

Printed in Hong Kong
16/THK/1

The publisher would like to thank everyone who worked to make
this book come together: Kate Olesin, project editor; Christina Ascani,
photo editor; Michaela Weglinski, editorial assistant; Anne LeongSon,
production assistant; Grace Hill, managing editor; Joan Gossett,
production editor; Christina Wilsdon, fact checker; Robert Johnston,
history consultant; and Kelsey Carlson, education consultant.

CONTENTS

FOREWORD

If you would not be forgotten
As soon as you are dead and rotten
Either write things worth reading
Or do things worth writing.

—Benjamin Franklin

FRANKLIN DID LOTS OF THINGS WORTH WRITING. He built a business in Philadelphia—his adopted home town—that furnished a good living for his family and good jobs to the people who worked for him. He published a newspaper, the *Pennsylvania Gazette,* which informed its many readers of the important events of their day. He invented the lightning rod, which kept people safe from lightning strikes, and the Franklin stove, which kept them warm during the winter. He helped establish a library, allowing people who couldn't afford books to borrow them, and a college, which provided education to young people. He served on the committee that drafted the Declaration of Independence. He arranged the alliance with France that led to the American victory in the Revolutionary War. He took the leading part in negotiating the peace treaty that ended the war. And he offered sage advice in the convention that produced the American Constitution.

But it was the things Franklin wrote that have made him the best loved of the Founding Fathers. Franklin wrote letters that contain words of wisdom, essays and newspaper articles that showed his insight into the human character, and satires and spoofs that poked fun at the pretensions of the proud.

His most famous literary work was *Poor Richard's Almanack*. Almanacs were small books that included calendars and contained useful information about the seasons, the weather, the best times for planting crops and harvesting them, the most promising cures for illness in humans and animals, and many other topics of interest to their readers. Franklin's *Poor Richard's Almanack* did all this and gave a bonus: the jokes Franklin told and the sound advice he framed in good humor.

Franklin's humor and his advice were a big hit in his lifetime. His almanac was a best seller. And the advice lives on, as sound advice usually does. The humor holds up well, too, which is less common. "Fish and visitors stink in 3 days," Franklin wrote. Anyone who has kept fish or visitors too long knows just what he was talking about.

There's one other thing that makes Franklin's writing worth reading. He wrote in a simple, straightforward style. He could remember his life when he was young and loved to read anything he could lay his hands on. He wrote in a way that young people—people like himself as a boy—could understand. They could understand his words at the time he wrote them, and they can understand them now.

All of which guarantees that, though he has long been dead and rotten, he won't be soon forgotten.

—>>>•●•<<<—

H. W. BRANDS has been teaching American history to high school and college students for 35 years. He has been writing about American history for almost that long. And Benjamin Franklin is one of his favorite subjects. His book *The First American: The Life and Times of Benjamin Franklin* was a finalist for the Pulitzer Prize.

THINK INNOCENTLY AND JUSTLY; AND IF YOU SPEAK, SPEAK ACCORDINGLY.

—*Benjamin Franklin*

→→→◄ In other words ... ►◄◄←

TRUST THE GOOD
IN OTHER PEOPLE.
BE FAIR TO EVERYONE IN YOUR THINKING AND SPEAKING.

O F ALL THE AMERICANS WHO EVER LIVED, Ben Franklin is one of the most interesting. Even though he only went to school until he was 10 years old, he kept reading and learning and eventually became famous as a scientist, inventor, statesman, and writer of many wise words. He seemed to enjoy just being alive and trying all kinds of new things. He loved to swim, play jokes on his friends, do scientific experiments, and come up with ideas for new projects. He didn't mind moving to a new city and starting a new life. In fact, he lived in some of the most important cities in the world—Boston, Philadelphia, London, and Paris.

Ben thought hard about the best ways to live so that he could be a good person, enjoy life, and accomplish a lot every day. He owned a printing company when he lived in Philadelphia, and he wrote funny stories and clever sayings in newspapers in an annual almanac he published. Sometimes Ben was just repeating a saying he liked that he had read or heard—about how to live well and smartly—but other times, he came up with his very own wise words. Many of the sayings Ben wrote or said are still quoted today.

Even things we have in our lives today came from ideas Ben had or projects he started—like wood-burning stoves, libraries, and hospitals. Sometimes people call Ben "the First American," because he had so many of the important qualities we think of as American. He believed people were equal, no matter how much money they had or what their social status was. And he believed in being resourceful. He was sure that if you thought about problems or projects that needed to be done, you could come up with ways to improve just about anything. And that's a pretty wise way to live.

1

TRANQUILITY

FIGURING OUT
THE THINGS
THAT
REALLY
MAKE US HAPPY.

A TRUE FRIEND IS THE BEST POSSESSION.

THERE'S NOTHING
BETTER IN LIFE
THAN A BEST BUD OR TWO
TO HANG OUT WITH.

—>>>•●•<<<—

DURING HIS LONG LIFE, BEN MADE ALL KINDS OF FRIENDS—
from shoemakers and landladies to important people in
government and science. In all the different places he
lived—in the United States, France, and England—he made
friends and kept them by staying in touch. In those days,
that meant letter writing. No cell phones, texting, or email in
BF's day.

One of his best pen pals was his sister Jane. Her life was very
different from Ben's. Jane had 12 children, and she spent her
days cooking, cleaning, taking care of her kids—and writing
letters now and then to her famous brother, Ben.

When Ben and Jane were young, the family called them Benny
and Jenny, and they were true friends. Ben taught his little sister
to write. That was usually something only the daughters of
gentlemen were taught back then. BF probably didn't realize at
the time that teaching Jane to write meant he would have a pen
pal for life.

CONTENT MAKES POOR MEN RICH; DISCONTENT MAKES RICH MEN POOR.

BEN THOUGHT BEING HAPPY
AND LIKING YOUR LIFE WAS A BETTER (AND RICHER) WAY TO LIVE
THAN SPENDING YOUR TIME AND ENERGY
COUNTING MONEY.

—➤➤➤•●•◀◀◀—

BEN SPENT A LOT OF TIME, EVEN AS A BOY, thinking about the best way to live so that he could get to his real goal—contentment. When he was young, he read a little book called *Essays to Do Good,* and it changed his life.

It said that even a poor man might have the wisdom to "save a city" or "serve a nation!" That probably made little Ben feel really happy, knowing that a boy like him could make a difference and do great things. And BF did! He came up with all kinds of good ideas for his city, Philadelphia, and for the new country—the U.S.A. That's why we call him a Founding Father.

TIME IS AN HERB THAT CURES ALL DISEASES.

EVER HEARD THE SAYING
"TIME CURES ALL ILLS?"
THIS IS THE SAME THING. WHEN YOU FEEL MAD OR SAD, JUST STEP BACK AND GIVE YOURSELF A LITTLE TIME.
OFTEN THE BAD FEELINGS WILL GO AWAY
OR FEEL A LOT LESS BAD.

—➤➤➤•●•❰❰❰—

I N THIS SAYING, BEN COMPARED TIME TO AN HERB, because in his day, a lot of people used herbal concoctions as medicine. His own mother-in-law sold a popular herbal remedy for itching called Widow Read's Ointment.

BF didn't think much of the doctors back then, and, really, they didn't have much scientific knowledge. They didn't know about germs, and they thought that bleeding patients—draining some of their blood—might cure them of "impurities."

A European man named Franz Anton Mesmer claimed he could cure all kinds of problems by changing a person's "magnetic fluids"—whatever that meant! He used chanting, light, and hypnosis in his treatment. Dr. Mesmer even treated the great composer Mozart and the French queen. But BF and some French scientists looked into Dr. Mesmer's cure and declared that it was just nonsense.

WITHOUT VIRTUE MAN CAN HAVE NO HAPPINESS IN THIS WORLD.

THE ONLY WAY TO BE HAPPY IS TO
BE A VIRTUOUS PERSON
AND THAT MEANS DOING WHAT YOU KNOW IS RIGHT,
EVEN WHEN IT'S HARD TO DO.

—————→ >>•‹‹‹—

MOST OF AMERICA WAS STILL WILDERNESS IN BEN'S DAY—wilderness that had been home to Native Americans for hundreds of years. But the colonists thought they could just claim those lands and settle them, and naturally that caused some pretty tense times.

In the early 1760s, fighting broke out between the new settlers and the Ottawa and Susquehannock tribes. Skirmishes went on until December 1763, when frontiersmen massacred about 20 defenseless Native Americans.

Ben was furious when he heard about the killings. He took up his pen, his favorite weapon. "The guilt will lie on the whole land till justice is done on the murderers," he wrote in a pamphlet that circulated through the colony. Not much justice was ever done then, but Ben had at least followed his own conscience.

EAT TO PLEASE THYSELF, BUT DRESS TO PLEASE OTHERS.

EATING IS SOMETHING THAT
JUST CONCERNS YOU,
SO EAT WHAT YOU LIKE (AS LONG AS IT'S HEALTHY).
BUT WHEN YOU'RE OUT WITH OTHER PEOPLE,
IT'S A GOOD THING TO CONSIDER
HOW THEY'LL FEEL ABOUT YOUR DRESS, YOUR TALK,
YOUR GENERAL DOINGS.

BY THE TIME THE REVOLUTION CAME, BF was a famous man, even in Europe. So the Continental Congress sent the great Benjamin Franklin to Paris to try to get the French king to support America's fight for independence.

Ben was 70 years old by then, and in France he started wearing very "American" clothes—sometimes leather jackets (because Native Americans wore them) and a little hat made of fur, to keep his head warm. The French loved Ben's style! They liked the idea of a "natural man," and they were sure BF *was* one. When Ben saw how much they liked his fur hat, he ordered more from America, to be sure he had a good supply.

While Ben was in Paris, a lot of French families admired him so much that they even had an engraving of "Doctor Franklin"—as they called him—hanging over their fireplace.

A LONG LIFE MAY NOT BE GOOD ENOUGH, BUT A GOOD LIFE IS LONG ENOUGH.

NO REASON TO SIT AROUND AND WONDER
JUST HOW
LONG YOU'LL LIVE.
CRAM EVERY DAY WITH THE GOOD STUFF—
GOOD TALK, GOOD WORK, GOOD TIMES.

—›—›—›—•—‹—‹—‹—

BEN WAS BRILLIANT AT LIVING A GOOD LIFE, and he also lived a long one. When he finally sailed back to America from France for the last time, he was almost 80 years old but still having fun. The trip across the Atlantic took about seven weeks, because 18th-century ships relied on the wind to get them where they were going. But Ben spent those weeks doing what he liked best—making scientific observations and coming up with ideas for new inventions.

He trailed a kind of thermometer he had made from an empty bottle behind the ship. That allowed him to take water temperatures for a project he had started years before—a map of the Gulf Stream, the warm ocean current that runs like a river on top of the North Atlantic Ocean. And he came up with an idea using cut-up playing cards to figure out how to study the way wind affected the ships' sails.

THE DESIRE OF HAPPINESS IN GENERAL IS SO NATURAL TO US, THAT ALL THE WORLD ARE IN PURSUIT OF IT.

EVERYBODY WANTS TO BE HAPPY.
SO THINK HARD ABOUT WHAT REALLY BRINGS YOU HAPPINESS, THEN GO FOR IT.

—→ >>→ •●• ‹‹← —

WE'VE ALL HEARD THE WORDS "the pursuit of happiness." They're right in the beginning of the Declaration of Independence. But where did the Declaration come from? Here's what happened.

In the hot summer of 1776, the Continental Congress decided to tell King George that the American colonies were going to separate from Britain. Five members of the Congress were appointed to write this declaration to the king. Thomas Jefferson, John Adams, and Ben Franklin were all on the committee, along with a couple of other men.

The committee decided Jefferson should do the writing. He showed his drafts to the others. BF thought it was fine and only made a few changes. John Adams made a few, too. Then the Continental Congress made some changes and agreed to the Declaration of Independence on July 4, 1776. That's why we celebrate the Fourth of July as Independence Day.

2

INDUSTRY

HOW TO GET
THE JOB DONE,
IN SPORTS,
SCHOOL,
AND LIFE.

THERE ARE NO GAINS WITHOUT PAINS.

TODAY WE SAY
"NO PAIN, NO GAIN,"
PARTICULARLY WHEN WE'RE TOUGHING IT
OUT TO GET IN SHAPE FOR SOMETHING
IMPORTANT WE'RE GOING TO DO,
LIKE SING IN A CONCERT, PERFORM IN A PLAY, OR PLAY IN A BIG GAME.

—→>>>•●•<<<—

BEN'S SPORT WAS SWIMMING. He worked hard to become a strong swimmer, even though swimming wasn't something most people did back then. His love for swimming really paid off one day, when something incredible happened in the water. When BF was a boy, he was flying his kite by a pond, and he decided to go for a dip. But he also really wanted to fly that kite. So he jumped out of the water, grabbed the kite, and got back in. When the wind started tugging on the kite, it tugged on Ben as well, and suddenly he was sailing across the pond under wind power.

Later, when Ben was in London as a young man, one man offered to give him money to start a swimming school, but being a swim instructor wasn't what BF had planned for his life.

EACH DAY LET DUTY CONSTANTLY BE DONE.

BEING DUTIFUL WAS A BIG DEAL IN BEN'S DAY.
THINGS WERE A LITTLE HARSHER BACK THEN,
BUT IT'S STILL A GOOD IDEA
TO DO WHAT YOU
SAY YOU'LL DO
AND WHAT PEOPLE COUNT ON YOU TO DO.

—⟩⟩⟩•●•⟨⟨⟨—

WHEN BEN WAS JUST 12, his father indentured him to his older brother James, who was a printer. That meant for nine years, Ben had to work as James's apprentice, learning how to set type. There were no computers in those days, just metal letters attached to small wooden blocks. Ben had to spell out each word to be printed in a newspaper or book with those block letters. Ben did his duty for five long years.

Then he got so tired of how James treated him that he ran away and ended up in Philadelphia. Later, the brothers became friends again, and when Ben had his own printing business, James's son became his apprentice.

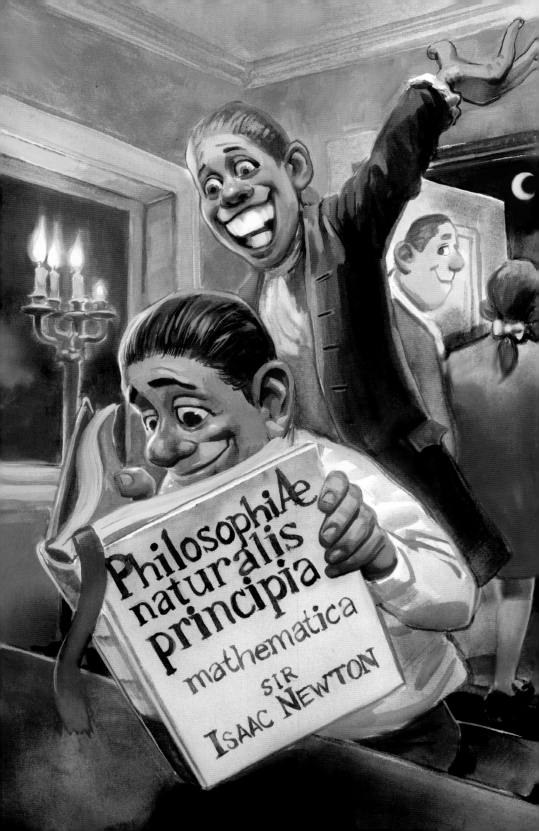

READ MUCH, BUT NOT MANY BOOKS.

READING BOOKS IS ONE WAY TO LEARN, BUT ACTUALLY GETTING OUT THERE AND EXPERIENCING THE REAL WORLD CAN TEACH YOU A WHOLE LOT, TOO.

—>>>•●•<<<—

BF WAS WHAT WE CALL AN AUTODIDACT—A SELF-LEARNER. He only went to school till he was 10 and started working right after that, first for his cousin, learning to make and repair knives, then for his brother as an apprentice printer. But Ben also kept reading, too. He was living in an exciting time, with lots of new ideas, especially about science. Before that, most people believed in religion or magic and superstition as a way to explain why things happened the way they did. Science was a whole new way of thinking about the world, and it began to change people's lives in amazing ways.

Remember how BF loved to fly a kite when he was a boy? Well, electricity became his passion when he was about 40 years old. No one really knew how it worked, so Ben began thinking about it as a form of energy, and he tried various experiments to prove that it was. He also believed that the water in thunderclouds was electrified. So he flew a kite on a wire string and that attracted an electrical charge, in a lightning storm. It was dangerous, so don't try it! Ben's experiments made him one of the most famous scientists in the world!

IF YOU WILL NOT HEAR REASON, SHE'LL SURELY RAP YOUR KNUCKLES.

TAKE TIME TO THINK BEFORE YOU ACT.
THINKING SOMETHING THROUGH BEFORE
YOU START DOING IT
MAKES THINGS GO A LOT SMOOTHER.

—⟩⟩⟩•●•⟨⟨⟨—

AFTER AMERICA WON THE REVOLUTIONARY WAR, the states hadn't really reasoned together a way to make a good government for the country. There were fights about who controlled rivers and how to fund an army. So in 1787, delegates from 12 of the 13 states met in Philadelphia to work on a constitution.

BF was 81 by then and living in Philadelphia again. It was painful for him to get out and about, so he sat in a chair attached to four poles, and four men put those poles on their shoulders and carried ole Ben to the convention. The delegates argued a lot, and BF often added a voice of reason and compromise that helped smooth things along. Finally, everyone agreed on the Constitution we have today.

IF YOU WOULD HAVE A FAITHFUL SERVANT, AND ONE THAT YOU LIKE, SERVE YOURSELF.

THE VERY BEST PERSON TO RELY ON IS YOURSELF.

JUST DO WHAT NEEDS TO BE DONE AND DON'T EXPECT SOMEBODY ELSE—YOUR MOTHER OR YOUR FATHER, MAYBE?—

TO DO IT FOR YOU.

—➤➤➤•●•❮❮❮—

I N BEN'S DAY, WELL-TO-DO PEOPLE HAD SERVANTS, and slaves. In the South, there were a lot of slaves—humans owned by other humans. In fact, Ben owned three slaves himself. One of them, named Peter, was his personal servant. But BF became more and more convinced that slavery was a real evil, and after the Revolution, he became an abolitionist—someone who thought all slaves should be freed.

People of the Quaker religion in Philadelphia had started the first group of abolitionists just as the Revolution began, and in 1787 Ben became the group's president. The group wanted to free all slaves and offer them an education.

Like Ben, other leaders in his era knew that slavery went against the very idea behind America—that all people are created equal. But sadly, America kept the institution of slavery for another 75 years or so, and it took another war, the Civil War, before all slaves were free.

A PAIR OF GOOD EARS WILL DRAIN DRY AN HUNDRED TONGUES.

MANY OF US LIKE TO TALK,
SO WE LIKE A GOOD LISTENER.
IT TAKES SOME WORK, BUT IF YOU TEACH YOURSELF TO BE A GOOD LISTENER,
YOU CAN LEARN A LOT.

———›››•—•‹‹‹———

BF KNEW THAT ONE OF THE BEST WAYS to earn someone's trust and respect was just by listening. He learned if he listened hard to friends, or even enemies, they would talk and talk, and he could figure out what got them worked up and what made them happy. It was a great skill to have as a friend, a diplomat, and a Founding Father.

Ben was a real genius at listening and then getting people to compromise. He did that at the Constitutional Convention in Philadelphia. The convention was about to fall apart because the states couldn't agree on some important things—like how many representatives each state should get. Then Ben proposed that each state get two senators, and that's what we have in the U.S. Senate today.

WELL DONE IS BETTER THAN WELL SAID.

EVER HEARD THE SAYING

"ACTIONS SPEAK LOUDER THAN WORDS"? SAME THING. BETTER TO BE A HARDWORKING DOER THAN A BIG TALKER.

———›››•●•‹‹‹———

THE BRITS WERE PRETTY BIG TALKERS when the Revolution started. Britain was the most powerful nation in the world, a real superpower, with colonies all around the globe and an amazing navy. The British king, George III, and most of his British subjects thought they could put the American troublemakers back in their place pretty quickly. Ben was actually in London when the tensions started, and he heard some of their big talk.

Nobody in America was talking big about how easy it would be to win the war. But they did keep fighting it—for six and a half long, hard years. Then finally in Yorktown, Virginia, the British got beaten so badly that they knew they had lost the war. October 19, 1781, was a great day for America.

3

ORDER

BEING CAREFUL AND
THOUGHTFUL
ABOUT WHAT YOU
SAY AND DO
MAKES
EVERYTHING EASIER.

A SLIP OF THE FOOT YOU MAY SOON RECOVER: BUT A SLIP OF THE TONGUE YOU MAY NEVER GET OVER.

BE CAREFUL WHAT YOU SAY.
BECAUSE ONCE IT'S SAID,
YOU CAN'T TAKE IT BACK—EVER.

—›››•●•‹‹‹—

SOMETIMES WHEN BEN WAS YOUNG, he said things he wished he hadn't. Maybe that's why he started writing a funny column for his brother's newspaper about a made-up character named Silence Dogood. Maybe her name was a reminder that being silent was like doing good.

BF also made up characters named Caelia Shortface, Anthony Afterwit, and Alice Addertongue. An adder is a snake with a venomous bite, and that was Alice, too! She liked to collect gossip and pass it on to anybody who would listen. If you made a slip of the tongue to Alice, she'd be sure to tell everyone.

Ben used all those characters to make fun of people in his world whom he thought were ridiculous or unfair, whether it was religious leaders, government officials, or just silly people.

'TIS EASIER TO PREVENT BAD HABITS THAN TO BREAK THEM.

WE'VE ALL GOT SOME BAD HABITS,
BUT WHEN YOU KNOW SOMETHING'S STARTING TO BE A PROBLEM—
WHETHER IT'S EATING TOO MUCH, TALKING TOO MUCH, OR TEXTING ALL THE TIME,
JUST STOP.

—>>>·●·<<<—

WHEN BEN WAS ONLY 18, he went to London on his own and lived there for about a year and a half. He settled into his new life, working as a printer, and made new friends. Like most people in London, his friends drank a lot of beer—a big glass before breakfast, one with their meals, and then four more before the day was over.

People drank beer or cider then because drinking water could make you sick. It wasn't filtered the way water is today. But beer drinking became one of those "bad habits" that BF decided to avoid. He liked to drink hot gruel—a kind of watery cereal (yuck!)—instead of beer.

HE THAT LIES DOWN WITH DOGS, SHALL RISE UP WITH FLEAS.

WHEN YOU HANG AROUND WITH SOMEONE, **THEIR WAYS AND IDEAS** WILL RUB OFF ON YOU.

——⟩⟩⟩•●•⟨⟨⟨——

BEN TRIED TO AVOID SHADY HUMAN CHARACTERS, but he couldn't avoid fleas, head lice, and all kinds of flying pests. People didn't have air conditioners or screens in colonial days, so in the summer when they opened the windows, mosquitoes and gnats came right in. When the Continental Congress was meeting in BF's own city, Philadelphia, in the summer of 1776, the flies "swarmed thick and fierce," Thomas Jefferson said.

TJ was trying to write the Declaration of Independence then, but those pesky flies kept landing on his legs and "biting hard" right through his silk stockings.

Other insects ate up the crops farmers grew to feed their families, so kids were often sent into the fields to pick the insects, one by one, off the crops.

HASTE MAKES WASTE.

IF YOU RUSH THROUGH
SOMETHING JUST TO GET IT DONE,
YOU MAY NOT DO IT RIGHT,
AND THEN YOU'LL HAVE TO DO IT
ALL OVER AGAIN.

—>>>•‹‹‹—

EVEN WHEN HE WAS A BOY, Ben was careful about doing his work well. When he grew up, he did his work so well and was such a success that when he was just 42, he could afford to stop his printing business and do what he wanted—which was to study the new ideas in science. He understood then more than ever that science takes slow, careful thinking and that experiments take time to do well.

Here's where his careful scientific thinking got him: He came up with ideas about electrical currents, the flow of the Gulf Stream, how to track the course of a storm, and how Earth's climate could change. And remember, he didn't even go to high school! So he didn't learn in the classroom. Instead, Ben taught himself science by reading and writing letters to other great scientists, mostly in Europe. People then and people now think BF was probably the greatest scientist of his day.

LET ALL YOUR THINGS HAVE THEIR PLACES; LET EACH PART OF YOUR BUSINESS HAVE ITS TIME.

STAY FOCUSED ON WHAT YOU'RE DOING.

WHEN IT'S TIME TO DO YOUR HOMEWORK, DO IT!

WHEN IT'S TIME TO EAT,

PAY ATTENTION TO THE FOOD AND COMPANY

(INSTEAD OF SNEAKING A LOOK
AT YOUR MESSAGES).

—→→→•●•◄◄◄—

THAT'S HOW **BF** MADE A SUCCESS OF HIS LIFE. When it was time to work, he worked. When it was time to have fun, he knew how to do that. In Paris, Ben was a big hit at gatherings—the Parisians called their evening parties "salons." But when it was time to get down to business and be serious with the Parisians, he knew how to leave the jokes behind.

When Ben came home to Philadelphia for the last time, he was almost 80, but he was still taking care of business and starting new ventures. He even became president of the Pennsylvania Executive Council, kind of like being the governor of the state.

A MAN IN A PASSION RIDES A MAD HORSE.

THIS JUST MEANS DON'T LET YOUR
EMOTIONS RUN AWAY WITH YOU,
BECAUSE THAT'S ONLY GOING
TO LEAD TO TROUBLE.

—›—›—›——●——‹—‹—‹—

ACTUALLY, THERE WAS ONE PATRIOT WHO NEEDED A HORSE THAT would run away with him—as fast as it could go. That was Paul Revere. He was a Son of Liberty, a group in Boston that was standing up to the British even before the Revolution started.

After a while, the British got fed up with the "Sons" and decided to send out troops to capture their leaders. When Paul learned which way the troops were headed, he made a famous midnight ride to warn people the British were coming.

BF was crossing the Atlantic when Paul Revere made his night-time ride. Ben had been living in London and was coming back to join the patriotic cause. People in Pennsylvania—and in the other colonies—were excited that Benjamin Franklin was coming home to be on the patriots' side.

AVOID TRIFLING CONVERSATION.

DITCH THE SILLY CHATTER
AND TALK ABOUT
STUFF THAT MATTERS.

—>>>•●•<<<—

BF ALWAYS LIKED GOOD CONVERSATION, especially talking about books, new ideas, and ways to make life better. Once he became a prosperous printer in Philadelphia, he started a men's club called the Junto to talk about important topics. Members weren't allowed to argue; they had to keep things polite.

Before a gentleman could join the Junto, he had to answer four questions: Was there anyone already in the group he didn't respect? Did he love his fellow humans, regardless of their religion or their profession? Should people be harmed for their opinions—about God or anything else? Did he love truth? You can guess what the answers needed to be.

4

HUMILITY

NOT ACTING LIKE YOU'RE BETTER THAN OTHER PEOPLE.

THOSE WHO ARE FEAR'D, ARE HATED.

YOU KNOW HOW EVERYBODY'S AFRAID
OF THE CLASS BULLY,
BUT REALLY, NOBODY LIKES HIM OR HER.
MAKING PEOPLE AFRAID
OF YOU IS JUST
NO WAY TO MAKE FRIENDS.

—⟶≫≻•●•≺≪⟵—

THE COLONISTS IN AMERICA HAD ALWAYS BEEN PROUD to be Britons and proud of their king. They almost thought of the king as a father to them—someone who wanted to keep them safe and secure. But then a new king, George III, was crowned in 1761, and he started acting like a bully.

BF was in London for the big coronation of the new, young king. George was only 23 years old and didn't really know how to rule an empire that stretched from India to America.

When the colonists in America began protesting about new taxes the British said they had to pay, George got mad instead of listening and trying to find a solution. "Once these rebels have felt a smart blow," he said, "they will submit." But he was wrong. The colonists weren't about to be bullied, and that's why the Revolution started.

BE TO THY PARENTS AN OBEDIENT SON [OR DAUGHTER].

IT'S ALWAYS A GOOD IDEA
TO RESPECT THE RULES YOUR PARENTS
SET FOR YOU.

—›—›—›—•—●—•—‹—‹—‹—

BEN HAD THREE CHILDREN OF HIS OWN, two boys and a girl. When his oldest son, William, was young, he and Ben got along just fine. William even helped him with his kite-flying experiment.

But when the Revolution began, William remained loyal to Britain, even though his dad tried to talk him into joining the patriotic fight for independence. In fact, William was the king's governor in New Jersey and worked against the patriots. So the Americans declared him "an enemy to the liberties of this country" and kept him imprisoned for almost three years.

After America won its independence, William wasn't welcome in the new United States, and he moved to England. Ben only saw him once after that, but their visit didn't go very well, and the two were never close again.

HE THAT CANNOT OBEY, CANNOT COMMAND.

IF YOU DON'T KNOW HOW TO TAKE ORDERS FROM THE PERSON IN CHARGE, YOU'LL NEVER MAKE A GOOD LEADER YOURSELF.

—→>>>•●•<<<—

BEN'S BROTHER JAMES SOMETIMES HAD A HARD TIME obeying orders from other people he didn't like or respect—especially the Puritan leaders in Boston. But he had no problem ordering his 12-year-old apprentice Ben around. Sometimes, he even beat Ben.

When James published articles in his newspaper attacking some of the Puritan leaders and other important people in the colony, the Massachusetts court ordered him to stop, but he wouldn't. He went to jail for a little while, but he told Ben to keep writing the troublesome articles.

Ben started to worry that he'd get in trouble too, and he had had enough of James's disrespect. He left the apprenticeship. But James told all the other printers in Boston not to hire his younger brother. That's when Ben sailed away. He arrived in Philadelphia hungry, dirty, and with almost no money. Still, going there was one of the best moves he ever made.

SEARCH OTHERS FOR THEIR VIRTUES, THY SELF FOR THY VICES.

LOOK FOR THE
GOOD STUFF IN OTHER PEOPLE,
BUT CHECK YOURSELF FOR WAYS
YOU COULD IMPROVE.

SINCE **B**EN BELIEVED IN VIRTUE AND SELF-IMPROVEMENT, he probably liked living in Philadelphia. People of the Quaker religion had founded the city, and even though Ben wasn't religious like the Quakers were, they practiced many of the virtues that Ben believed in. They were friendly, worked hard, practiced humility, and treated other people as equals.

Quakers even called their religion the Society of Friends. They were tolerant of other religions, too, so people of other faiths came to Philadelphia to live. Even the name of the city itself means "brotherly love."

In Ben's day, the Quakers used a way of talking called "plain speech." They said "thou" instead of "you" and "thy" instead of "your." Maybe that's why Ben wrote this saying with "thy" in it.

GREAT BEAUTY, GREAT STRENGTH, AND GREAT RICHES ARE REALLY AND TRULY OF NO GREAT USE; A RIGHT HEART EXCEEDS ALL.

LIVING A RIGHTEOUS LIFE AND
BEING A GOOD PERSON
ARE MORE IMPORTANT THAN
BEAUTY, STRENGTH, AND WEALTH.
BUT YOU NEED TO FIGURE OUT FOR YOURSELF
WHAT BEING GOOD MEANS.

—→→→•●•←←←—

BF ALWAYS LIKED TO THINK THINGS THROUGH, and he wanted to live with "a right heart." He was raised as a Puritan. Puritans believe in living a holy life with God at its center. For a while, Ben's father wanted him to be a Puritan minister. But when he grew up, Ben gave up being a Puritan and didn't go to any church at all. Instead, he read the beliefs of a lot of different religions.

He also allowed himself quiet time for his own devotions. He even wrote something he could use for that quiet time called *Articles of Belief and Acts of Religion.* It had songs, prayers, and readings that he found inspiring.

Later in his life, he told a friend that he believed in one God, who had created the universe. He also believed God was kind and ought to be worshipped and that the best way to serve him was to do good to other humans.

NEVER GIVE WAY TO SLOTH, OR LUST, OR PRIDE.

DON'T BE SLOTHFUL—LAZY.
DON'T LET YOUR LUSTS—
THINGS YOU WANT REALLY BADLY—
RUN AWAY WITH YOU.
AND DON'T BE PROUD—
THINKING YOU'RE BETTER
THAN OTHER PEOPLE.

—>>>•●•<<<—

HERE'S A FUNNY STORY. Ben thought that the bald eagle was a lazy, sloppy bird. He said he wished it "had not been chosen as the Representative of our Country.

"He is a Bird of bad moral Character. He does not get his Living honestly. You may have seen him perch'd on some dead Tree near the River, where, too lazy to fish for himself, he watches the Labour of the Fishing Hawk; and when that diligent Bird has at length taken a Fish, and is bearing it to his Nest for the Support of his Mate and young Ones, the Bald Eagle pursues him and takes it from him."

BF liked the wild turkey a lot better than the eagle, because even though the turkey was "a little vain and silly," he was "a Bird of Courage," and he wasn't lazy like the eagle.

DON'T THROW STONES AT YOUR NEIGHBOURS, IF YOUR OWN WINDOWS ARE GLASS.

IT MAY SEEM EASY TO
"THROW STONES"—MAKE FUN OF OR
CRITICIZE OTHER PEOPLE—
BUT EACH OF US HAS THINGS
PEOPLE COULD MAKE FUN OF, TOO.

—⟫⟩⟩ •●• ⟨⟨⟨—

BEN UNDERSTOOD THAT A LOT OF PEOPLE get their kicks from talking trash about other people, because "it gives us the satisfaction of making ourselves appear better than others," he once wrote, "or others no better than ourselves." But he also decided that was a pretty rotten way to live.

When Ben made his second voyage across the Atlantic, coming home from his first visit to London, he made a list of the new ways he would act. One of the items on his list said: "I resolve to speak ill of no man whatever, not even in a matter of truth." Instead, he planned to "speak all the good I know of every body." Ben was 20 years old then, but he seems to have followed that plan pretty closely for most of his life.

5

RESOLUTION

HANG IN THERE,
KEEP AT IT,
AND YOU'LL
GET WHAT
YOU'RE AFTER.

DILIGENCE IS THE MOTHER OF GOOD LUCK.

DILIGENCE MEANS NOT GIVING UP—

AT WHATEVER YOU'RE DOING.

AND IF YOU DON'T GIVE UP,

YOU'LL PROBABLY HAVE PRETTY GOOD LUCK

WITH WHATEVER YOU WANT TO DO.

—➤➤➤•●•◀◀◀—

BEN'S FATHER, JOSIAH, REALLY BELIEVED IN DILIGENCE, and he taught it to all 13 of his children. Josiah was a part of a religious group called the Puritans, who had come to Boston from England. Boston was part of the Massachusetts Bay Colony, founded by the Puritans in 1630, and was meant to be a place where all Puritans would be free to practice their religion, because in England Puritans were sometimes persecuted for their beliefs.

Josiah's favorite expression was from the Bible, and it promised that a person who was diligent in his calling—his work—would "stand before Kings." After Josiah died, Ben had this carved on his father's gravestone: "Diligence in thy calling."

Like his father, Ben also believed in diligence. Still, when he was young, he never dreamed he would actually stand before kings. But, guess what—Benjamin Franklin stood before five kings in his lifetime!

RESOLVE TO PERFORM WHAT YOU OUGHT. PERFORM WITHOUT FAIL WHAT YOU RESOLVE.

DECIDE WHAT
THE RIGHT THING TO DO IS,
AND THEN DO IT!

—→•>→•—•—•<•<•<—

THAT'S WHAT THE LEADERS OF THE AMERICAN PATRIOTS DID. When King George and the British Parliament kept making laws that were unfair to them, the patriots' leaders met at the Continental Congress and decided they would have to tell the king they wouldn't stand for it anymore. They declared America independent from Britain. That was a dangerous thing to do in those days, and they all knew it. It took courage, but they were willing to risk everything for freedom.

Ben said to them, "We must, indeed, all hang together, or most assuredly, we, indeed, shall all hang separately." He meant that all the patriots needed to stick together and support each other in the coming fight, or they could literally be hanged by the British, one by one.

BE NOT DISTURBED AT TRIFLES, OR AT ACCIDENTS COMMON OR UNAVOIDABLE.

EVER HEARD THE EXPRESSION

"DON'T SWEAT THE SMALL STUFF"?

THAT'S WHAT THIS MEANS.

WE ALL HAVE LITTLE ACCIDENTS,

LIKE BREAKING A GLASS OR FORGETTING SOMETHING.

SO DON'T WORRY ABOUT IT.

—→ ⇒ ⟫ • ◆ • ⟪ ⇐ ←—

IN THE COLONIAL ERA, one thing people did have to worry about were accidents with fire. Kitchens had big, open fire-places, where a couple of fires might be burning at the same time. That could be pretty dangerous, and so were the candles that people used to light their houses.

There were no fire departments back then. So Ben organized a firefighting club in Philadelphia and called it the Union Fire Company. BF wrote the rules for members, and they even got together for dinner once a month to discuss their ideas about fires and how to fight them. When there was a fire in town, fire company members would grab their own buckets and race to help. Ben was one of the brave men who helped put out fires in his town. He even had his own leather buckets stamped with "B. Franklin & Co."

'TIS NEVER TOO LATE TO MEND.

ANYTIME IS A GOOD TIME TO MEND A RELATIONSHIP BY SAYING YOU'RE SORRY OR MENDING YOUR WAYS, WHICH MEANS CHANGING THINGS YOU DO THAT BOTHER OTHER PEOPLE.

—→ ›››•●•‹‹‹—

BEN WROTE THIS SAYING IN A LETTER he sent to a London newspaper in 1773, when he was living there. He had a lot of British friends who were important and who respected him, but Ben was losing respect for the way the king and the British government were treating the American colonies. He said in his letter that government officials should admit they were wrong and mend their ways. He signed the letter, "A sincere Well-wisher to GREAT BRITAIN and her Colonies. B. Franklin."

If the British had just listened to Ben! If they had stopped taxing Americans so much and stopped bullying them, then there probably wouldn't have been a Revolutionary War. And who knows? America might still be part of Britain!

LITTLE STROKES FELL GREAT OAKS.

WHEN YOU'VE GOT
A BIG JOB AHEAD OF YOU,
START WITH LITTLE STEPS,
AND BEFORE YOU KNOW IT,
IT WILL BE DONE.

—→ ›››› •●• ‹‹‹‹ ←—

IMAGINE HOW THE PATRIOTS FELT when they decided to fight the Revolution. That was a superhuman job. Britain was a "great Oak," for sure. It was the most powerful nation in the world, with a strong army and great navy to fight the colonists.

And the redcoats won a lot of the early battles. But then General George Washington and his army started winning some—making little strokes against Britain. Finally, after six and a half years and more than a hundred battles, the Americans brought the great oak, Britain, down.

Ben and other patriots hoped the Revolution in America would change the way people everywhere saw government. They wanted everybody—not just kings and the powerful—to have more say in how things were run and how people were allowed to live their lives. "We are fighting for the dignity and happiness of human nature," Ben said.

LEARN OF THE SKILLFUL: HE THAT TEACHES HIMSELF, HATH A FOOL FOR HIS MASTER.

THERE ARE A LOT OF SMART PEOPLE OUT THERE
READY TO TEACH US ALL THEY KNOW.
ALL WE HAVE TO DO IS PAY ATTENTION AND BE WILLING TO LEARN.

—›››•●•‹‹‹—

THERE WEREN'T PUBLIC SCHOOLS IN AMERICA back then, so kids learned in other ways. Some were home-schooled or had a tutor. A lot of people lived on farms, so parents taught their kids how to plant a crop, milk a cow, and spin wool or flax into fabric for clothes.

If you wanted to learn a trade, like being a silversmith, you became an apprentice to an older silversmith, who would teach you how to make teapots, knives, forks, and other things. One silversmith in Ben's hometown of Boston, Paul Revere, was also a patriot. In 1775, he made a famous "midnight ride" to warn other patriots that British soldiers were coming after them.

Ben learned how to be a printer by becoming his brother's apprentice, and it suited him, since printers in those days were also writers who published their own newspapers and pamphlets. As you can tell by now, Ben soon became a fine writer.

YOU MAY DELAY, BUT TIME WILL NOT.

DON'T PROCRASTINATE—
PUT OFF DOING WHAT YOU NEED TO DO—
BECAUSE, AS ANOTHER SAYING GOES,
"TIME MARCHES ON,"
WHETHER YOU ARE IN STEP WITH IT OR NOT.

—⟶ ⟫⟫ •●• ⟪⟪ ⟵—

BEN WANTED TO TAKE ADVANTAGE OF TIME as much as he could and live a full life. He was always thinking of ways to do that. One way was to go to bed early and get up early.

He wrote a funny essay in Paris about how people there should get up earlier, and many years later, some Americans read that essay and came up with the idea of Daylight Saving Time that we have today.

One night each spring, we all set our clocks forward one hour, so it seems like it's an hour later but it's still light outside. Daylight Saving Time helps us have more hours of daylight on spring and summer evenings. This year, when you or your parents set the clocks forward, you can think of ole Ben Franklin.

NOTHING DRIES SOONER THAN A TEAR.

WHEN YOU FEEL SAD
OR DISAPPOINTED,
REMEMBER THAT IT PROBABLY WON'T
LAST THAT LONG.

—>>>•‹‹‹—

BF WASN'T ONE TO TALK ABOUT BEING SAD or disappointed, but he had times when he felt that way. One of those times might have been when he was about 11 or 12 years old. He really wanted to do what lots of Boston boys did around that age—sign up with one of the sailing ships in Boston Harbor and go to sea.

The smell of the sea filled the Boston air, and Ben spent a lot of time on the waterfront, dreaming about sailing to foreign lands. One of his brothers had done that, but Ben's father absolutely did not want BF to spend his life sailing the seas. So he didn't become a sailor. But later in his life, when he was living in London and Paris, he did travel back and forth across the ocean between America and Europe many times. Maybe those voyages reminded him of his boyhood dream of going to sea.

FIVE MINUTES LATER...

6

SINCERITY

WAYS TO
KEEP IT REAL
AND
KEEP IT
HONEST.

HONESTY IS THE BEST POLICY.

ALWAYS STICK TO
WHAT'S TRUE
AND MAKE SURE
YOU'RE HONEST WITH YOURSELF.

—→→⊱•●•⊰←←—

WHEN HE WAS A BOY, BF was already a leader among his friends. He and his buds liked to fish for minnows— tiny fish—in a salt marsh near their homes. But standing in the marsh made a muddy mess, so Ben had the idea to build a stone fishing wharf.

There was a pile of stones nearby that workers were using to build a new house. After the workers left one evening, Ben got his friends together and carried some of the stones to the marsh and built their little fishing wharf. Bad idea. When Ben's father learned BF had taken the stones without asking, Ben told him that building the wharf had been "useful work." But Ben's dad said that "nothing was useful that was not honest."

MEN AND MELONS ARE HARD TO KNOW.

YOU CAN'T KNOW WHAT
A CANTALOUPE OR WATERMELON
WILL BE LIKE INSIDE BY LOOKING AT IT.
THE SAME GOES
FOR PEOPLE.

—→→→•●•←←←—

THINK OF ALL THE DIFFERENT KINDS OF PEOPLE Ben got to know in his long life (he lived to be 84). He knew Puritans and Quakers, rich folks and poor folks, the colonists in America, British politicians, and French aristocrats. He got to know famous scientists, soldiers, diplomats, and even kings.

How did Ben become friends with people from so many different cultures, religions, social classes, and occupations? Probably by watching and listening and figuring out what mattered to them. Ben was a genius at a lot of things, but one of his best talents was getting to know other people.

OH 'TIS EASIER TO KEEP A HOLIDAY, THAN COMMANDMENTS.

A LOT OF THE HOLIDAYS
STARTED FOR
RELIGIOUS REASONS,
BUT WE FORGET TO CELEBRATE THE MEANING
AND MORALS BEHIND THEM.

—➤➤➤•●•❮❮❮—

BEN FOLLOWED UP THIS THOUGHT BY SAYING that a lot of people observe Christ's birthday, Christmas, but not his teachings. Jesus taught that it was "more blessed to give than to receive," so that's a good one to keep in mind on holidays—and every day, no matter what religion you practice!

When Ben was a boy in Boston, he probably never celebrated Christmas. The Puritans didn't believe in celebrating it. In Philadelphia, where he lived next, the Quakers who had founded the colony of Pennsylvania felt the same way. But some other Philadelphians sang carols and celebrated with turkey dinners.

In 1776, America got a big Christmas gift. That night it was pelting snow, but George Washington's army crossed the icy Delaware River not far from Philadelphia, and the next morning surprised the enemy in Trenton. It wasn't a big battle, but it gave Americans hope that maybe the Revolution wasn't lost after all.

TART WORDS MAKE NO FRIENDS: A SPOONFUL OF HONEY WILL CATCH MORE FLIES THAN A GALLON OF VINEGAR.

THERE'S NO REASON

TO BE SOMEONE WHO ARGUES OR MAKES FUN OF OTHER PEOPLE.

A NASTY TONGUE ONLY TURNS PEOPLE AWAY.

IF YOUR TALK IS FRIENDLY,

YOU'LL HAVE MANY MORE FRIENDS.

—→ >>•●•<< ←—

BEN WROTE AN AUTOBIOGRAPHY— the story of his life— explaining the good and bad things that happened to him. In it, he said that when he was a teenager, he liked to argue and debate with people and win the argument. But then he stopped talking that way. He decided it would be better to express himself with a "modest Diffidence," meaning he stopped talking as if he was always right.

BF wrote in his autobiography that his new way of talking was a "great Advantage" to him for the rest of his life, because it helped him persuade people to do the things he hoped they would. He thought know-it-alls turned other people off. What do you think? Ben's autobiography is a short book, but it's famous. In fact, for a long time, kids in school were required to read it, and it's still a great book to read!

WHAT YOU WOULD SEEM TO BE, BE REALLY.

DON'T BE
A FAKE.
JUST BE WHO YOU REALLY ARE.

—›››•●•‹‹‹—

BF WAS A VERY REAL GUY. He never tried to be like someone else or put on airs. Even when he became famous, he didn't act like he was cooler than other people.

He tried to explain to his son William how important it is to be yourself. In fact, the first part of Ben's autobiography is written in the form of letters to William. But William ignored Ben's wise words.

When William was a young man, Ben sent him to study law in London. While William was there, he liked hanging out with British noblemen in their fancy homes. One of his favorite books was *The True Conduct of Persons of Quality*. William always wanted to be a big, important "man of quality" and feel like he was better than other people. When he became the royal governor of New Jersey, he lived in his own fancy house and people called him "Excellency." He liked that.

A FALSE FRIEND AND A SHADOW, ATTEND ONLY WHILE THE SUN SHINES.

A GOOD FRIEND WILL
BE THERE FOR YOU IN ALL KINDS OF WEATHER—
MEANING WHEN YOU'RE HAPPY AND SUNNY
AND WHEN YOU'RE
SAD OR GLOOMY.

—⫸⫸•●•⫷⫷—

WHEN BEN WAS AN APPRENTICE, he made friends with another smart teenager, John Collins. The two liked to debate with each other. John even followed Ben to Philadelphia after Ben settled there. But as time went on, John began to resent Ben and became pretty obnoxious.

One day, when John was with Ben and some other guys out rowing on a river, he got mad when Ben said John had to row like everybody else. He even tried to push Ben in the river, but Ben threw him overboard instead. John was okay, but that was the end of the friendship.

Ben had a couple of false friends in his life, but he didn't let that bother him. He didn't hold a grudge against people who hadn't been true friends.

7

>>>•<<<

MODERATION

DON'T
OVERDO THINGS;
LESS IS
USUALLY
MORE.

EAT TO LIVE, AND NOT LIVE TO EAT.

SOME PEOPLE CAN'T STOP
THINKING ABOUT FOOD.
IT'S THE MAIN THING ON THEIR MINDS.
BUT, REALLY, FOOD IS FOR FUELING YOUR BODY,
AND KEEPING YOU HEALTHY,
NOT FOR FIXATING ON.

—›—›—›—•—●—•—‹—‹—‹—

WHEN BF WAS ABOUT 16 and an apprentice to his brother, he decided to become a vegetarian. Some nights, for dinner Ben just ate a biscuit or a slice of bread or a tart and a handful of raisins. Those were the days before people knew how to eat a healthy vegetarian diet, but Ben said he felt good eating his new diet.

He did that for about a year; then while on a sailing trip to New York, the crew caught some codfish. "When the fish were opened up, I saw smaller fish taken out of their stomachs," Ben later wrote. "Then thought I, 'If you eat one another, I don't see why we mayn't eat you.'" And that was the beginning of the end of his vegetarian days!

FISH AND VISITORS STINK IN 3 DAYS.

YOU KIND OF HAD TO LIVE IN BEN'S TIME
TO GET THIS SAYING, BUT IT JUST MEANS THAT
VISITORS SHOULDN'T OVERSTAY THEIR WELCOME
OR TAKE ADVANTAGE
OF THEIR HOST'S GENEROSITY.

—→-➤➤-•●•-◄◄-←—

REMEMBER THAT IN **BF'S** DAY, there were no refrigerators. Fresh fish or meat didn't keep for long before they spoiled and began to stink—though sometimes people caked meat and fish in salt or dried them to keep them longer.

Visitors who stayed too long probably didn't stink, despite what Ben says. But Ben did have an uncle who came to stay with the Franklin family when Ben was young. The uncle stayed for four years! That didn't make Ben's dad very happy, so maybe that's why BF came up with this saying.

In colonial times, most people who came to visit with friends and relatives stayed for more than three days, though, despite Ben's saying. Travel was really hard back then. There were no cars, no trains, no planes, not even bicycles! If you took a long trip, you had to rely on a horse to get you where you wanted to go. And after a long, bumpy ride in a carriage, in a wagon, or on horseback, you wanted to stay for a while and visit.

FOR WANT OF A NAIL THE SHOE WAS LOST; FOR WANT OF A SHOE THE HORSE WAS LOST; AND FOR WANT OF A HORSE THE RIDER WAS LOST ...

PAY ATTENTION TO THE LITTLE THINGS, **BECAUSE IF YOU DON'T, THEY CAN LEAD TO BIGGER PROBLEMS. SAY YOU FORGET TO STUDY FOR A TEST AND YOU GET A BAD SCORE—THAT ONE EXAM COULD BRING YOUR GRADE DOWN FOR THE WHOLE YEAR.**

—➤➤➤•●•◄◄◄—

IF YOU'VE NEVER RIDDEN A HORSE, you may not know that a lot of horses wear shoes! Not the kinds we wear, but metal ones in the shape of their hooves. The horseshoes are nailed into the hooves to protect a horse's feet, so they're a good thing.

Ben quoted this saying in one of his editions of *Poor Richard's Almanack*. Every year from 1732 to 1757, he published a new version of this best seller. The *Almanack* had predictions about the weather and the stars and a calendar for the coming year. It also had a lot of wise sayings just like this one, which is just a variation on a proverb that had been around for hundreds of years before Ben put his own spin on it.

EARLY TO BED AND EARLY TO RISE, MAKES A MAN HEALTHY, WEALTHY, AND WISE.

BEST TO GET TO BED EARLY
AND GET UP EARLY, AND
YOU'LL FEEL BETTER AND DO BETTER
AT EVERYTHING.

—→·→·→·•·◦·←·←·←—

WHEN BEN WAS IN PARIS, he had lots of Parisian friends who liked to party late into the night and then sleep until noon, with their curtains drawn. So, BF wrote a funny piece about that for the local newspapers.

In the essay, BF said one morning he got up early for a change, and a strange light was shining outside. It was the sun! He acted like he was amazed to learn that it rose hours before noon! Who knew! Here was a way to save money on all those candles that you needed to light your house late into the night, he wrote. Go to bed earlier and get up earlier, and use the morning sunlight to get things done.

HE THAT CAN HAVE PATIENCE, CAN HAVE WHAT HE WILL.

DON'T GET RESTLESS AND GIVE UP. **IF YOU WAIT OR WORK HARD FOR SOMETHING YOU WANT, YOU'VE GOT A MUCH BETTER CHANCE OF GETTING IT.**

—→>>·●·<<←—

AS YOU CAN TELL, BEN ALWAYS HAD BIG IDEAS, and he learned to be patient about getting them accomplished. One of those ideas was to form a "library company." In the colonial days, libraries in America were private ones, usually in rich people's houses. But Ben loved to read and wanted to make books available to lots of people. So he suggested to some of his fellow book lovers that they each donate a little money to buy books they could share.

It took BF about a year to raise enough money to order books, wait for them to arrive, and rent a small room for them. Finally, in 1731, the Library Company of America opened in Philadelphia. It inspired people to start other public libraries all over America, and it's still around today.

A PENNY SAV'D IS TWOPENCE CLEAR.

SAVING MONEY THAT COMES YOUR WAY
IS THE BEST WAY TO HAVE MONEY.
ONCE YOU SPEND YOUR CASH, IT'S GONE,
AND SOMETIMES WE SPEND MONEY ON
SOMETHING THAT CATCHES OUR EYE THAT MOMENT,
BUT THAT WE DON'T REALLY NEED,
OR EVEN WANT.

—➤➤➤•●•◄◄◄—

BEFORE THE REVOLUTION, colonies issued their own coins, and people even used foreign coins, like Spanish pieces of eight. There was no official American money.

That came after the Revolution, and the first American coin, minted in 1787, was the penny. Guess who suggested the design on it? That's right, Benjamin Franklin! It was made all of copper, and it was much larger and heavier than our pennies today. One side said "United States" wrapped around the words "We are one." A drawing of a chain with 13 links, representing the 13 original states, encircled the words. The other side of the coin showed a sun shining on a sundial with these words under it: "Mind your business." Doesn't that sound just like BF?

BE SLOW IN CHUSING A FRIEND, SLOWER IN CHANGING.

YOU KNOW HOW SOMETIMES YOU MEET
A NEW PERSON AND YOU
BECOME "FAST FRIENDS,"
BUT AFTER A WHILE, THE FRIENDSHIP DOESN'T WORK ANYMORE?
BEST TO BE SURE ABOUT SOMEONE BEFORE
MAKING THEM A GOOD FRIEND,
THEN STICK WITH THE FRIENDSHIP.

—▸ ▸▸ •●• ◂◂ ◂—

BEN HAD A LOT OF CASUAL FRIENDS, but he was careful about making close friends. One man who became a true friend was Thomas Jefferson. While BF was in Paris working as an American diplomat, TJ was sent to help him with his work. The two had known each other from their days on the Continental Congress in Philadelphia, but in Paris they became good friends. It was natural that they would really like each other, because they were both scientists and inventors and philosophers. In fact, they were both geniuses.

When Ben died years later, Jefferson called him "our great and dear friend, whom time will be making greater." Time did make Ben great, and his wisdom helped America get its start. When we read his wise words, it almost makes us feel like we know him as our own great and dear friend.

BEN'S BIG IDEAS AND AMAZING INVENTIONS

BENJAMIN FRANKLIN LEFT HIS MARK ON SO MUCH OF AMERICA. In ways you don't even think about, you or your family or friends are probably still benefiting from ideas Ben had.

GLASS ARMONICA

This is a really fun musical instrument. If you've ever run a wet finger around the top of a glass and heard it "sing," you have some clue as to what an armonica sounds like. Ben's armonica had 37 different-size glass bowls, with a spindle, a pedal, and a flywheel to "ring" them. It made very unusual music!

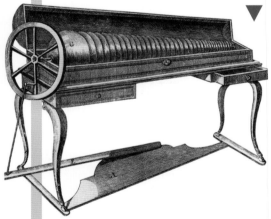

BIFOCAL GLASSES

Ben called these "double spectacles," but really they were one pair of glasses. The top half of the lenses helped improve distance vision, and the bottom half helped with reading and up-close work.

COLLEGE

There were only a few colleges in America when Ben proposed an academy in Philadelphia. In 1751, this was the first college not attached to any religion. His academy later became the University of Pennsylvania, still a great institution.

FRANKLIN STOVE ▶

You can still buy one of these stoves named after Ben today. His was a metal-lined, wood-burning stove that could be put inside fireplaces. The stove drew up cool air from the basement and heated it, then released it through vents into the room. It was a much more efficient way to heat than an open fireplace.

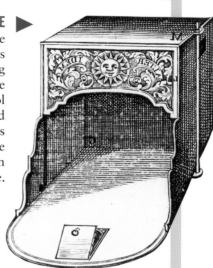

▲ ELECTRICITY

Ben didn't "invent" it, but he discovered that it flowed from one object to another, like a liquid does. Once he understood that, he came up with the idea for lightning rods. People put these on the roofs of their houses, so that if lightning struck, it would hit the rod and travel down a wire to the ground. That kept the electric current from setting the house on fire.

SWIM PADDLES

Ben used kites to pull him across a pond when he was a boy. He also came up with swimming paddles for each hand that he could hook his thumb through and big sandal-like flippers for his feet, so he could speed through the water when he swam.

HOSPITAL

In 1751, Ben and a doctor friend of his named Thomas Bond started America's first hospital, the Pennsylvania Hospital. It is still around today.

▼

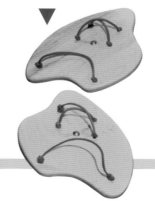

BIBLIOGRAPHY AND RESOURCES

For a timeline of Franklin's life, go to www.ushistory.org/franklin/info/timeline.htm.

For Franklin's collected papers, see franklinpapers.org/franklin.

For Franklin's involvement in the American Revolution, see the following link to the Library of Congress exhibit, "Benjamin Franklin: In His Own Words": www.loc.gov/exhibits/franklin/franklin-cause.html.

For Franklin's many contributions to civic and political life, see www.pbs.org/benfranklin/l3_citizen_founding.html and www.archives.gov/exhibits/charters/constitution_founding_fathers_pennsylvania.html.

For Franklin's friendships, see the following article by historian Robert Middlekauff: www.washingtonpost.com/wp-srv/style/longterm/books/chap1/benjaminfranklinandhisenemies.htm.

For Franklin's relationship with his sister, Jane, see www.npr.org/2013/10/10/231431080/meet-bens-sister-jane-historys-forgotten-franklin.

For daily life in the colonial era, visit Colonial Williamsburg's extensive website: www.history.org.

Brands, H. W. *The First American: The Life and Times of Benjamin Franklin.* Doubleday, 2000.

Franklin, Benjamin. *The Autobiography and Other Writings.* Viking Penguin, 1986.

Franklin, Benjamin. *Benjamin Franklin's The Art of Virtue: His Formula for Successful Living,* Ed. George L. Rogers. Foster & Foster, 1996.

Franklin, Benjamin. *Wit and Wisdom.* Peter Pauper Press, 1998.

Humes, James C. *The Wit & Wisdom of Benjamin Franklin.* HarperCollins, 1995.

Isaacson, Walter. *Benjamin Franklin: An American Life.* Simon & Schuster, 2003.

Kostyal, K. M. *Founding Fathers: The Fight for Freedom and the Birth of American Liberty.* National Geographic, 2014.

Lepore, Jill. *Book of Ages: The Life and Opinions of Jane Franklin.* Vintage, 2014.

Waldstreicher, David. *Runaway America: Benjamin Franklin, Slavery, and the American Revolution.* Hill & Wang, 2005.

SOURCE NOTES

PAGE 8 ... think innocently and justly; and if you speak, speak accordingly. *Autobiography of Benjamin Franklin, Part 9;* **PAGE 13** A true Friend is the best Possession. *Poor Richard's Almanack, 1744;* **PAGE 14** Content makes poor men rich; Discontent makes rich Men poor. *Poor Richard's Almanack, 1749;* **PAGE 17** Time is an herb that cures all Diseases. *Poor Richard's Almanack, 1738;* **PAGE 18** ... without Virtue Man can have no Happiness in this World ... *Articles of Belief and Acts of Religion, November 20, 1728;* **PAGE 21** Eat to please thyself, but dress to please others. *Poor Richard's Almanack, 1739;* **PAGE 22** A long Life may not be good enough, but a good Life is long enough. *Poor Richard's Almanack, 1755;* **PAGE 25** The desire of happiness in general is so natural to us, that all the world are in pursuit of it. *Memoirs of Benjamin Franklin, vol. 11;* **PAGE 29** There are no Gains without Pains. *Poor Richard's Almanack, 1758;* **PAGE 30** Each Day let Duty constantly be Done. Acrostic from Benjamin Franklin (the Elder) MS *Commonplace Book of Benjamin Franklin (the Elder):* American Antiquarian Society, Sent To B.F. in N.E. 15 July 1710; **PAGE 33** Read much, but not many Books. *Poor Richard's Almanack, 1738;* **PAGE 34** ... if you will not hear Reason, she'll surely rap your Knuckles. *Poor Richard's Almanack, 1758;* **PAGE 37**

If you would have a faithful Servant, and one that you like, serve yourself. *Poor Richard's Almanack, 1758;* **PAGE 38** A Pair of good Ears will drain dry an hundred Tongues. *Poor Richard's Almanack, 1753;* **PAGE 41** Well done is better than well said. *Poor Richard's Almanack, 1737;* **PAGE 45** A Slip of the Foot you may soon recover: But a Slip of the Tongue you may never get over. *Poor Richard's Almanack, 1747;* **PAGE 46** 'Tis easier to prevent bad habits than to break them. *Poor Richard's Almanack, 1745;* **PAGE 49** He that lies down with Dogs, shall rise up with fleas. *Poor Richard's Almanack, 1733;* **PAGE 50** Haste makes Waste. *Poor Richard's Almanack, 1753;* **PAGE 53** Let all your Things have their Places. Let each Part of your Business have its Time. *Autobiography of Benjamin Franklin, Part 9;* **PAGE 54** A Man in a Passion rides a mad Horse. *Poor Richard's Almanack, 1749;* **PAGE 57** Avoid trifling Conversation. *Autobiography of Benjamin Franklin, Part 9;* **PAGE 61** Those who are fear'd, are hated. *Poor Richard's Almanack, 1744;* **PAGE 62** Be to thy parents an Obedient son [or daughter]. Acrostic from Benjamin Franklin (the Elder) MS *Commonplace Book of Benjamin Franklin (the Elder):* American Antiquarian Society, Sent To B.F. in N.E. 15 July 1710; **PAGE 65** He that cannot obey, cannot command. *Poor Richard's Almanack, 1734;* **PAGE 66** Search others for their virtues, thy self for thy vices. *Poor Richard's Almanack, 1738;* **PAGE 69** Great Beauty, great strength, and great Riches are really and truly of no great use; a right Heart exceeds all. *Poor Richard's Almanack, 1739;* **PAGE 70** Never give Way to sloth or lust or pride ... Acrostic from Benjamin Franklin (the Elder) MS *Commonplace Book of Benjamin Franklin (the Elder):* American Antiquarian Society, Sent To B.F. in N.E. 15 July 1710; **PAGE 73** Don't throw stones at your neighbours, if your own Windows are glass. *Poor Richard's Almanack, 1736;* **PAGE 77** ... Diligence is the Mother of Good luck ... *Poor Richard's Almanack, 1758;* **PAGE 78** Resolve to perform what you ought. Perform without fail what you resolve. *Autobiography of Benjamin Franklin, Part 9;* **PAGE 81** Be not disturbed at Trifles, or at Accidents common or unavoidable. *Autobiography of Benjamin Franklin, Part 9;* **PAGE 82** ... 'tis never too late to mend ... Printed in *The Public Advertiser*, September 14, 1773; **PAGE 85** ...Little Strokes fell great Oaks. *Poor Richard's Almanack, 1758;* **PAGE 86** Learn of the skillful: He that teaches himself, hath a fool for his master. *Poor Richard's Almanack, 1741;* **PAGE 89** You may delay, but Time will not. *Poor Richard's Almanack, 1758;* **PAGE 90** Nothing dries sooner than a Tear. *Poor Richard's Almanack, 1757;* **PAGE 95** ...Honesty is the best Policy... [letter] To Edward Bridgen, Passy, Oct. 2. 1779; **PAGE 96** Men and Melons are hard to know. *Poor Richard's Almanack, 1733;* **PAGE 99** Oh 'tis easier to keep a holiday, than commandments. *Poor Richard's Almanack, 1743;* **PAGE 100** Tart Words make no Friends: a spoonful of honey will catch more flies than a Gallon of Vinegar. *Poor Richard's Almanack, 1744;* **PAGE 103** What you would seem to be, be really. *Poor Richard's Almanack, 1744;* **PAGE 104** A false Friend and a Shadow, attend only while the Sun shines. *Poor Richard's Almanack, 1756;* **PAGE 109** Eat to live, and not live to eat. *Poor Richard's Almanack, 1733;* **PAGE 110** Fish and visitors stink in 3 days. *Poor Richard's Almanack, 1736;* **PAGE 113** ... For want of a Nail the Shoe was lost; for want of a Shoe the Horse was lost; and for want of a Horse the Rider was lost ... *Poor Richard's Almanack, 1758;* **PAGE 114** ... Early to Bed and early to rise, makes a Man healthy, wealthy, and wise. *Poor Richard's Almanack, 1758;* **PAGE 117** He that can have Patience, can have what he will. *Poor Richard's Almanack, 1736;* **PAGE 118** A Penny sav'd is Twopence clear ... *Poor Richard's Almanack, 1737;* **PAGE 121** Be slow in chusing a Friend, slower in changing. *Poor Richard's Almanack, 1735.*

—➤➤➤•●•◀◀◀—

EDUCATIONAL EXTENSIONS: GRADE 6

1. Cite examples in the text of how Ben Franklin valued living a good life. What did he mean by "a good life"? How did he encourage others to do the same?

2. When the author calls Ben Franklin "resourceful" what does she mean? Cite examples in the text that you think demonstrate resourcefulness.

3. Pick one of Ben Franklin's quotes and explain how it relates to you or an experience in your life.

INDEX

Boldface indicates illustrations.

PHOTO CREDITS

122 (UP), Granger, NYC — All rights reserved; 122 (LO), Ted Thai/Getty Images; 122-123 (LO), Archive Photos/Getty Images; 123 (UP), Werner Wolff/Getty Images; 123 (UP LE), Granger, NYC — All rights reserved; 123 (LO RT), Denise Sanchez/Allentown Morning Call/MCT/Getty Images